Dedicated to
"Dallas, Donavan Jr. & Dane"

Mommy When I'm You, What Will I Do?

By AMBER MERRITT

*To: Miss NoLa Girl You're a Star ★
Amber Merritt 2020*

Inst@Amber.theauthor

All Rights Reserved. No part of this publication may be reproduced, stored in a retrieval system or transmitted in any form or by any means electronic, mechanical, photocopying, recording or otherwise, without the prior written permission of the publisher. Author/writer rights to "Freedom of Speech" protected by and with the "1st Amendment" of the Constitution of the United States of America. This is a work of fiction with grade school educational learning. Any resemblance to actual events, locales, person living or deceased that is not related to the author's literacy is entirely coincidental.

With this title/copyrights page, the reader is notified that any belief system, promotional motivations, including but not limited to the use of non-fictional/fictional characters and/or characteristics of this book, are within the boundaries of the author's own creativity in order to reflect the nature and concept of the book.

Any and all vending sales and distribution not permitted without full book cover and this copyright page.

Published by: Amber R. Merritt
Copyrights©2018 Amber R. Merritt, All Rights Reserved
Book Title: Mommy When I'm You, What Will I Do?
Date Published: 03.29.2019 / Edition 1 *Trade Paperback*
ISBN: 978-1-9851-3119-4
Illustrations by: Black Dollar Marketing
Arranged by: UR' Graphics Guy urgraphicsguy@gmail.com

SproutingSunflowers@gmail.com

This book was published in the United States of America.
Book Inspected and Accredited by: ASA Publishing Corporation

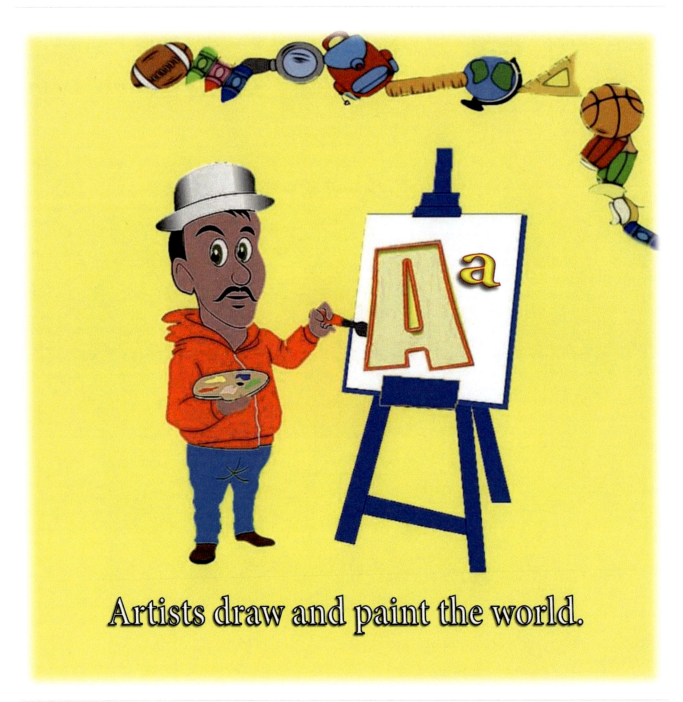
Artists draw and paint the world.

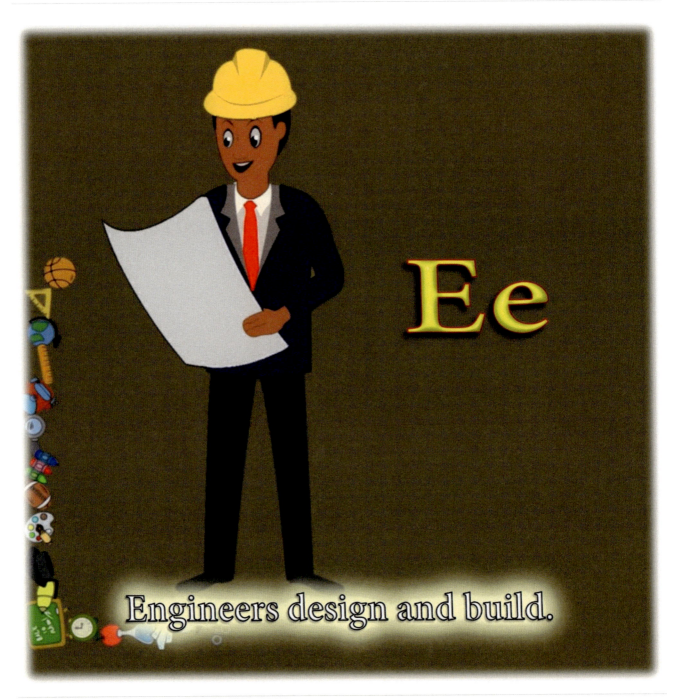

Ii

Interpreters are those of many languages.

Journalists,

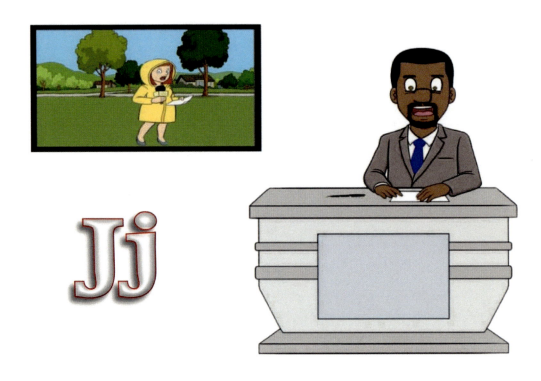

are there to cover the story whenever they get a call.

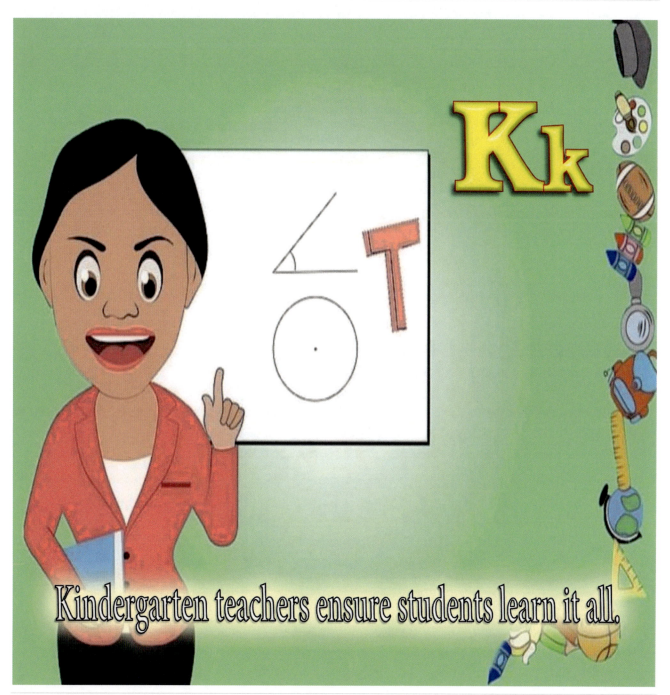

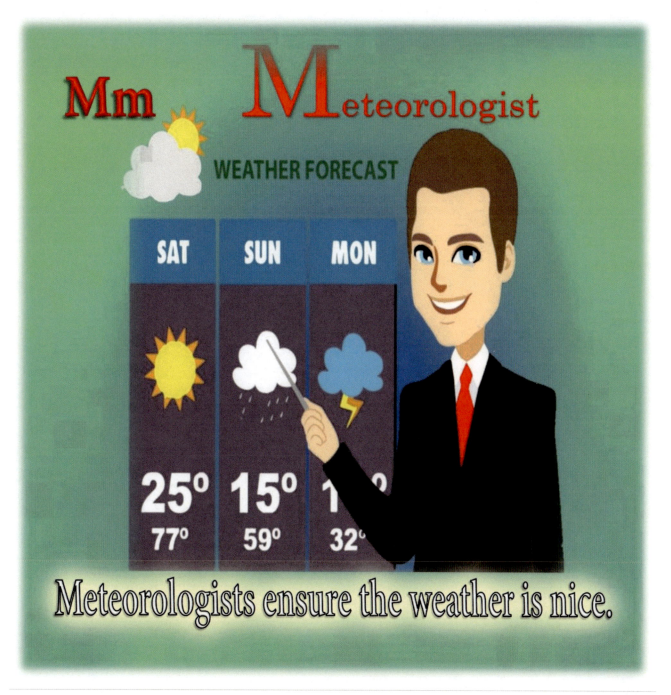

Uppercase Alphabets

A B C D E F G
H I J K L M N O P
Q R S T U V
W X Y Z

Lowercase Alphabets

a b c d e f g
h i j k l m n o p
q r s t u v
w x y z

Made in the USA
Monee, IL
01 March 2020